LANGUAGE
ARTS
EXPLORER
JUNIOR

How to Write a Play

by Cecilia Minden
and Kate Roth

CHERRY LAKE PUBLISHING · ANN ARBOR, MICHIGAN

CHERRY LAKE
Publishing

Published in the United States of America by Cherry Lake Publishing
Ann Arbor, Michigan
www.cherrylakepublishing.com

Content Adviser: Gail Dickinson, PhD, Associate Professor, Old Dominion University, Norfolk, Virginia

Photo Credits: Page 4, ©Igor Bulgarin/Shutterstock, Inc.; page 6, ©Ammit/Shutterstock, Inc.; page 9, ©Subbotina Anna/Shutterstock, Inc.

Library of Congress Cataloging-in-Publication Data
Minden, Cecilia.
How to write a play / by Cecilia Minden and Kate Roth.
p. cm. — (Language arts explorer junior)
Includes bibliographical references and index.
ISBN 978-1-61080-490-5 (lib. bdg.) —
ISBN 978-1-61080-577-3 (e-book) — ISBN 978-1-61080-664-0 (pbk.)
1. Playwriting—Juvenile literature. I. Roth, Kate. II. Title.
PN1661.M54 2012
808.2—dc23   2012010421

Cherry Lake Publishing would like to acknowledge the work of The Partnership for 21st Century Skills. Please visit www.21stcenturyskills.org for more information.

Printed in the United States of America
Corporate Graphics Inc.
July 2012
CLFA11

Table of Contents

Curtain Up!

Sometimes actors wear colorful costumes.

Like a good book, a play tells a story. Instead of reading the story, an **audience** watches live actors perform on a stage. The words the actors speak are written by a playwright. Plays are written in a format called a **script**. A script includes everything an actor needs to perform a role.

Scripts include:

- Time and **setting**: when and where the play takes place
- **Plot**: what happens in the play
- **Characters**: people acting in the play
- Stage directions: instructions to guide the actors as they perform
- **Dialogue**: words spoken by the actors

Plays have been around since the time of the ancient Greeks.

Do you have an idea for a play? Would you like to be a playwright? All you will need is a pencil, paper, and your imagination. Let's get started!

Miss Muffet and the Spider
By Mother Goose
SCENE ONE

(It is a pretty spring day in the park. MISS MUFFET enters from stage right. She is carrying a lunch box. She crosses to a park bench, sits, and looks around the park.)

MISS MUFFET: What a beautiful day to be outdoors! I think I will sit on this park bench and enjoy my nice lunch.

(SPIDER enters from stage left. He slowly creeps up behind the park bench and hides.)

MISS MUFFET: Oh, look! Mom packed a lunch of curds and whey, my favorite! I will eat my lunch and look at the birds and flowers.

(SPIDER jumps out from behind the park bench and yells loudly.)

SPIDER: Want to share your lunch with me, Miss Muffet?

MISS MUFFET: Oh my! Oh my!

The Big Race

Tortoises move very slowly.

Before you sit down to write a play, you need a story to tell. In this book, we'll base our play on a famous **fable**. *The Tortoise and the Hare* was written by Aesop (EE-sop), a famous Greek writer who lived thousands of years ago.

First, decide where and when the play will take place. For example, the story of the tortoise and the hare could take place on a country road on a hot summer morning. You could also set the play on a winter afternoon in a city. How would the play be different? Think about what you want to see on the stage. This will help guide your choices.

Second, decide what will happen during the play. In Aesop's fable, a hare challenges a tortoise to a race. Every play needs a **conflict**. In this fable, the conflict is between the tortoise and the hare. In the end, the tortoise wins the race because the hare takes a nap and doesn't wake up in time.

Conflict between the tortoise and the hare makes the story interesting.

Choose the Time, Setting, and Plot

In this activity, you will plan where and when the play takes place. You will also plan the conflict.

INSTRUCTIONS:
1. Write the title "Planning Sheet" on the top of your paper. You will be planning your play on this paper.
2. Make a list of possible settings for the story in your play. Include the place and time.
3. Plan the conflict that will occur in each setting. In one sentence, describe what will happen in the play.

PLANNING SHEET
- *Setting:* country road; *Time:* summer morning; *Plot:* hare challenges tortoise to a race
- *Setting:* city street; *Time:* winter afternoon; *Plot:* tortoise challenges hare to a race
- *Setting:* school yard; *Time:* morning recess; *Plot:* bully challenges another kid to a race

To get a copy of this activity, visit www.cherrylakepublishing.com/activities.

Enter the Tortoise and the Hare

Have you ever noticed that interesting characters make a movie more exciting?

Think of a movie you watched recently. It is likely that some characters in the movie were good and some were bad. For a play to work well, you need both good and bad characters. This creates the conflict. The characters need to be interesting to the audience.

Picture the characters in your mind. Imagine talking to them. How do they sound? What are their names? For example, what would you imagine a hare named Jack looks like? What if his name were Sylvester? Does he look different? Sound different?

Sometimes authors write a short biography of each character before they start writing the play. This is called a **character sketch**. This gives the actor ideas about how to act out the character on the stage.

ACTIVITY

Develop the Characters

In this activity, you will write a character sketch for each character.

INSTRUCTIONS:
1. Choose at least two characters for your play. Make one character bad. Make one good.
2. Write a list of characters on your Planning Sheet.
3. Write a character sketch for each character. How do they look? How do they sound when they speak?

To get a copy of this activity, visit www.cherrylakepublishing.com/activities.

Teddy Tortoise
- a plump, green tortoise
- takes his time when he walks
- likes to think a bit before he speaks
- is always kind to others
- speaks in a slow and careful manner

Jack Hare
- a slender, brown hare
- constantly moving
- likes to brag about his skills as a runner
- can be quite rude to others
- speaks in a quick and jumpy manner

11

How to Get to the Finish Line

Next, you will plot out your story. Plays are divided into **acts**. Each act tells you a little bit more about the story. Acts are sometimes divided into **scenes**. Within each scene, the main character may go to different places or talk to different people.

Think about the **timeline** and the conflict. What do you want to happen? How and when will it happen? Maybe the bad character wants to outdo the good character. For example, the hare wants to beat the tortoise in the race.

The first scene would set up the plot. The hare challenges the tortoise. The tortoise accepts. They agree on where to begin and end the race.

In the next scene, the hare is so sure he will win

that he takes a nap. The tortoise keeps walking. Include action to surprise the audience. All of the scenes should build to the final scene when the conflict is solved.

Act I, Scene I:

ACTIVITY

Build the Action

In this activity, you will plot out your story and begin to write your play.

INSTRUCTIONS:
1. On your Planning Sheet, write a timeline for your play. Write each action that will happen in order.
2. List which actions will happen in each act and each scene.
3. On a clean sheet of paper, begin to write your play by writing the settings for each scene.
4. Begin by writing "Act 1, Scene 1" and describing the setting.

Timeline for Tortoise and Hare

Act 1, Scene 1:
- A country road in a wooded area on a sunny summer day
- Teddy Tortoise is enjoying his picnic lunch.
- Jack Hare challenges Teddy to a race.
- Teddy accepts and begins to move toward the finish line.
- Jack takes a nap.

Act 2, Scene 2:
- Wooded area now has a finish line banner across the stage
- Teddy is almost at the finish line.
- Jack wakes up, begins to race, and then sees Teddy.
- Teddy crosses the finish line.

To get a copy of this activity, visit www.cherrylakepublishing.com/activities.

The Tortoise and The Hare

SCENE ONE

(It is a warm summer day in the forest. Animals are picnicking and playing games. HARE enters from off stage. He looks around at all the animals and then spies TORTOISE quietly eating his lunch near an old country road. HARE shows the audience a big smile and jumps over to TORTOISE.)

"I Can Beat You!"

The actors tell the audience the story of the play with dialogue. It takes practice to write good dialogue. The dialogue must sound natural to the characters. Think about how the character would react to the action and what he would say. Use your character sketches to help guide you.

Dialogue is written in a specific way. The name of the speaking character is written first, followed by a colon. The words the character will speak come next. Finally, there are stage directions written in parentheses. Here is an example:

HARE: I am so fast. I can beat anyone on this road. Tortoise, do you want to race?

TORTOISE: I will race you, Hare. I am slow but steady. I might not be first, but I always finish what I start.

(TORTOISE puts down his lunch box and begins to walk down the road.)

To get a copy of this activity, visit www.cherrylakepublishing.com/activities.

ACTIVITY

Write the Dialogue

In this activity, you will use your Planning Sheet to write the script.

INSTRUCTIONS:

1. Use the script you began in the last activity when you wrote the setting.
2. Write your story in the format of a play script. Use your Planning Sheet to help you turn your plot into dialogue and stage directions for your characters.
3. Make sure to write in the specific way of a play script—Character: dialogue, stage directions in parentheses.
4. Write your dialogue so your audience can hear how your characters sound when they are talking.
5. When you begin a new scene, remember to describe the setting for that scene. Then you can write the dialogue and stage directions.

I am so fast.

The Tortoise and The Hare

SCENE ONE

(It is a warm summer day in the forest. Animals are picnicking and playing games. HARE enters from stage left. He looks around at all the animals and then spies TORTOISE quietly eating his lunch near an old country road. HARE shows the audience a big smile and jumps over to TORTOISE.)

HARE: I am so fast. I can beat anyone on this road. Tortoise, do you want to race?

(HARE is jumping around, speaking loudly and in a bragging manner.)

TORTOISE: I will race you, Hare. I am slow but steady. I might not be first, but I always finish what I start.

HARE: I'm so sure I will win. I will let you go first. Let's race down the road to the big tree and back again.

TORTOISE: Thank you, Jack Hare, you are very kind. I think I can make it that far. I will start now so I will finish before the end of the day.

(TORTOISE puts down his lunch box and begins to walk down the road. He walks away from HARE very slowly.)

HARE: Ha-ha. The end of the day! I could run that race in a few minutes. Teddy Tortoise is so slow that I think I'll eat his lunch before I begin.

(HARE picks up TORTOISE's lunch box, dumps it out, and eats the rest of the lunch. He spies a piece of paper. He looks at the audience and smiles. He writes on the piece of paper. As he jumps around TORTOISE, he tapes the piece of paper to TORTOISE's back.)

TORTOISE: I thought you wanted to race, Jack Hare, but you haven't even started yet.

HARE: Oh, I have lots of time. In fact, I think I will take a little nap. You keep walking, and I will catch up later.

(TORTOISE turns around, and we see a sign that reads "Slow -Moving Vehicle" taped to his back. HARE rolls on the floor laughing. TORTOISE exits the stage, and HARE curls up for a long nap.)

And the Winner Is . . .

The end of the play is the most exciting part. It is called the climax of the play. The entire play has been building up to this part. You can put in a few twists and turns to make the audience think one way. Then you can end the play with a complete surprise. For example, a character the audience thought was bad might turn out to be good. You might want to try several different endings until you find one that pleases you.

To get a copy of this activity, visit www.cherrylakepublishing.com/activities.

ACTIVITY

Write the Climax

In this activity, you will write the final scene of your play.

INSTRUCTIONS:
1. Write the word "Climax" on your Planning Sheet.
2. Make a list of possible ways your story could end.
3. Continue adding to your script.
4. Write dialogue and stage directions to show how the conflict in your story is resolved.

Climax

- Hare wakes up and begins to race. Tortoise crosses the finish line before Hare.

- Hare wakes up and doesn't see Tortoise cross the finish line. He thinks the applause is for him.

- Hare is still asleep when Tortoise crosses the finish line.

SCENE TWO

(It is now afternoon. TORTOISE has walked all the way to the big tree and is on his way back. We can see him at the edge of the stage. HARE is waking up and yawning. The other animals have put up a finish line banner across the stage. They are waiting for TORTOISE to cross the line.)

HARE: What a good nap I had. Let's see, what was I doing? Oh, yes, I'm going to beat that slow Teddy Tortoise in a race. Guess I'll go run circles around him!

(HARE stands up and makes a big show of stretching and getting ready to run. TORTOISE continues to cross the stage very slowly. HARE is standing with his back to TORTOISE and the finish line, so he doesn't see him.)

HARE: I knew I could beat that slowpoke! He's probably still by the big tree, if he got that far! I bet he got lost going around the tree! Ha-ha, that is pretty funny. Getting lost going around a tree!

(TORTOISE continues to get closer and closer to the finish line, while HARE brags about winning. The other animals are cheering for TORTOISE, but HARE thinks they are cheering for him. The closer TORTOISE gets, the louder they cheer. HARE still thinks all the applause is for him.)

HARE: Thank you. Thank you. I know I'm the best runner in the forest! Well, here I go to win the race! See you in a few minutes!

(As he turns, he sees TORTOISE crossing the finish line. The other animals give a big cheer for TORTOISE.)

TORTOISE: I know I am slow, but I'm steady. I might not always be first, but I always finish what I start.

(HARE stands and stares while the other animals cheer for TORTOISE.)

THE END

Applause

STOP! DON'T WRITE IN THE BOOK!

ACTIVITY

Final Changes

Check everything one more time. Read your play aloud to hear how it sounds.

☐ YES ☐ NO Do I begin with the time and setting?

☐ YES ☐ NO Do I have a good plot?

☐ YES ☐ NO Do I have interesting characters?

☐ YES ☐ NO Do I have a conflict?

☐ YES ☐ NO Do I have an ending with a strong climax?

☐ YES ☐ NO Do I have different scenes?

☐ YES ☐ NO Does the dialogue sound natural?

☐ YES ☐ NO Do I have stage directions in parentheses?

☐ YES ☐ NO Do I use correct grammar and spelling?

After you've written your script, you can plan ways to put on your play for others. Be the director. Tell the actors how to act out your script. Then just wait for the applause!

Glossary

acts (AKTS) main divisions of a play

audience (AWD-ee-uhns) a group that watches or listens to a performance

characters (KAR-ik-turz) people in a made-up story or play

character sketch (KAR-ik-tur SKECH) a brief description of a character in a play

conflict (KAHN-flikt) a clash or disagreement that creates the action of a story

dialogue (DI-uh-lawg) words spoken by characters in a play

fable (FAY-buhl) a story that teaches a lesson

plot (PLAHT) the events of a play's story

scenes (SEENZ) divisions of a play act

script (SKRIPT) written text of a play

setting (SET-ing) where and when a story takes place

timeline (TIME-line) the order of actions in a play

For More Information

BOOK

Shepard, Aaron. *Folktales on Stage: Scripts for Reader's Theater*. Olympia, WA: Shepard Publications, 2006.

WEB SITE

Plays Magazine—Scripts for Young Actors

www.playsmagazine.com

A good source for scripts for young readers.

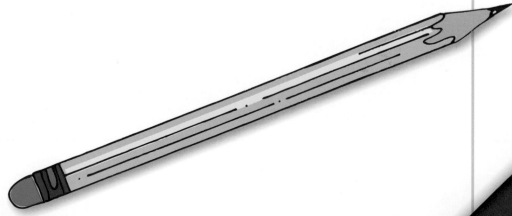

Index

About the Authors

Cecilia Minden, PhD, is the former Director of the Language and Literacy Program at Harvard Graduate School of Education. She earned her Doctorate from the University of Virginia. While at Harvard, Dr. Minden also taught several writing courses. Her research focused on early literacy skills and developing phonics curricula. Prior to becoming a professor, Dr. Minden was a professional actress and high school drama teacher. She is now an educational consultant and the author of more than 100 books for children. Dr. Minden lives with her family in Chapel Hill, North Carolina.

Kate Roth has a doctorate from Harvard University in language and literacy and a master's from Columbia University Teachers College in curriculum and teaching. Her work focuses on writing instruction in the primary grades. She has taught first grade, kindergarten, and Reading Recovery. She has also instructed hundreds of teachers from around the world in early literacy practices. She lives in Shanghai, China, with her husband and three children, ages 3, 7, and 10.